CHANGING
THE LIGHTBULB

CHANGING
THE LIGHTBULB

Seeking Recovery from the
Bondage of Self

NICHOLAS B.

To order additional copies of this book, contact:
Xlibris Corporation
1-888-795-4274
www.Xlibris.com
Orders@Xlibris.com
118720

CONTENTS

INTRODUCTION

WELCOME TO MY world, as I see it today. Compared to the way I have seen it from time to time in my drinking career, it is a beautiful place to live. With the exception of approximately six years of sobriety while I was raising my son, my life has been a constant struggle to achieve the impossible. The impossible in my case was to prove that I could have control over myself as far as drinking alcohol was concerned. The rest of the story is that I thought that by relying on my self I could somehow control other events in my life and when it turned out I could not, my pride prevented me from accepting it. These other events almost always involved other people.

Although alcohol was my drug of choice (make no mistake about it, alcohol is a drug), I dabbled in other substances with the same motive: to change or forget about the way I felt. I crossed the line into addiction at 13 years of age. My life was forever changed at that point, because I began to look at the world as a place to provide me with what I wanted when I wanted it. The fact that I found the effect of alcohol pleasurable made me determined to seek this effect over and over despite any consequences that came my way.

Some addicts progress into serious consequences more quickly than others, and the fact that my most serious came later rather than sooner in my drinking career served to prove in my own mind that I was unique. I never started drinking with the wish to lose every material possession, but this happened more than once. I didn't plan to lose jobs, watch a girlfriend die in front of me while binging with her, be confined in treatment programs, mental institutions, or jails. But these things happened to me as natural consequences of addiction. My own death would have been the end of it, of course. I have even told myself from time to time that death was preferable to the mental and physical anguish that I have experienced from my addiction. I was as imprisoned by my own mind as much as I became physically imprisoned as consequences for my actions. The only difference was that the self imprisonment began many years before my involuntary imprisonments.

Today, and just for today, I can understand why I am not dead as the result of my disease. Today I chose to quit fighting to gain control of my disease because of pride. Today I surrendered. Today the disease won, just as it did when I was 13 years old. I just refused to admit defeat at that time. The disease which is in me has won every battle. I just do not have to get into the ring with it today. And today that's OK with me. The fact that I have all the help I need, whenever I need it, makes recovery possible.

My opinions are my own, but nothing I could possibly say about addiction is original. Both the problem and the answer have been repeated endlessly. I have been in and out of recovery since 1988 and the message has always been the same. Much of the time I just didn't want to hear it because I wanted to rely on my own thinking. If you are an addict and things are going well in your recovery you already know what this book is about. You have had the "psychic change" which is sufficient to recover from a seemingly hopeless state of mind. You would get just as much out of going to a good meeting as you would from reading this book. If you are struggling there is something you have missed. While this book will not keep anyone sober, one more testimonial to the truth of the answer can't hurt.

Substance abuse addiction affects the mind, body, and spirit of the human animal. The way out begins in the spirit, which can begin the process to heal other areas. I used to feel sorry for myself because I did not ask to become an addict. This attitude kept me fighting the disease instead of accepting it. In fact, all my thinking and actions kept me in this disease I didn't ask for. You might say that I became heavily invested in fighting reality. I even spent a number of years arguing I didn't have the disease even though the evidence was over-whelming. Thank GOD my disease is treatable. Not all potentially fatal diseases can be treated. Today I know that I will die with my disease but do not have to die from it.

The thinking distortions that are present in all cases of substance abuse addiction have similar characteristics. Other addicts may have different life experiences, but the bondage of self is something that all substance abuse addicts have in common. These distortions cause problems because we do not respond to life situations in healthy ways. No amount of thinking distortion can change the realities of life.

This book is not an auto-biography although I use a few examples from my life experience of fighting reality instead of accepting it. There is a way out of our dilemma but we have to have a glimpse of reality and want to deal with it, not fight it. Dealing with life on life's terms for addicts requires a different kind of skill set than we can learn on our own. I hope that my take on our problem will serve that purpose. That is the way recovery from the bondage of self begins, with a little glimpse of reality.

One time while lying drunk I struggled mightily with changing a light bulb in a lamp beside my couch. I even went to the trouble of driving to Walmart in a drunken stupor to get a new bulb. When I found the plug halfway out of the socket and nothing wrong with the bulb I was furious with the whole situation. Getting the light to work did not make me feel any better.

I am just like the light bulb; I need to plug into a power source outside of myself in order to function.

NICHOLAS B.

CHAPTER 1

The Problem

T HE DRUGS THAT we addicts take give us a reward for using them. Whether this reward is to stimulate the pleasure pathway of the brain, make us forget the problems we think we have or do have, mask our true feelings, add excitement through loss of inhibitions, enhance our feeling of sensations, enable us to feel a part of like-minded groups, or all of the above, they work. All of these, together or in combination, seem like perfectly good reasons to start using a chemical. By the time the side effects in the form of consequences start catching up to us we are in no position to make a rational decision whether to use are not. Even if the consequences start out-weighing the rewards when looked at in a logical manner, real addicts have ceased thinking logically. Our investment in providing ourselves with the reward and our pride lead us to rationalize using again. We want the reward even if the side effects start becoming a bitch. We want the reward to the extent that we convince ourselves, (or can easily be convinced), that we can control the next situation that arises out of using. Most often we don't think there will even be more consequences, only the reward.

I think about this every time I see a prescription drug advertisement on TV. Sometimes the side effects sound worse than the condition they are supposed to treat. I can think about those ads somewhat objectively, why haven't I been able to do that in regard to my own using?

The answer is that I have permanently changed the basic way my brain functions by opening the Pandora's Box of the pleasure pathway. After making the decision to use, my self esteem is invested in what will happen. Since I was "in control" of my decision to use, the need to be right about my decision to use becomes as important to me as the actual use. How could I possibly be wrong about something that makes me feel so good? My pride and distorted thinking tells me not only can I not be wrong, but that anybody who has a problem with me using needs to mind their own business and stay out of mine. It's my life, right?

When I took some psychology classes in what now seems like a long time ago, I learned about the concept that people need to fulfill certain needs and that as these needs are met, they move on up the list of needs until they *self actualize*. Through this process a normal person builds self esteem, which is how worthy they feel.

We addicts screw this up royally. The need to feel that we can make our own decisions is there, but we can't do that because of the overwhelming need to get what we now want at the moment more that what we really need. As a result we often forego even the basic needs to get what we think we want. As our losses begin to mount up we rationalize by engaging in false or misplaced pride in a vain attempt to feel OK about our selves. We engage in denial that the consequences are all that bad, even if they take us into our own self made hell.

The fact that addicts have no chance to fulfill the normal progression of needs makes it hard to understand all the attention some psychologists and psychiatrists give to the addict's poor self esteem. With addiction there is no possibility for realistic self esteem because all of our resources are placed on the priority of what we think we need; the reward from a chemical. So

NICHOLAS B.

whatever issues we have or choose to use as excuses are irrelevant unless we can stay sober. Without sobriety any background issues remain and usually become worse. The one thing that the addict clings to throughout his or her ordeal is their own distorted sense of self worth. As the disease of addiction progresses, the thinking distortions of addicts move further away from reality in the form of false and misplaced pride so they can rationalize that what they are doing is OK. The selfish and self centered addict distorts both their perception and reactions to what the real world is doing to them in the form of logical consequences.

Addicts, by necessity must isolate into their own self centered world and the obvious way to do that is the way we relate to other people. By using inadequate strategies to deal with people based on our negative feelings, or by simply withdrawing from contact with other people, we isolate in order to use at will. People pleasing can be just as an inadequate strategy as open hostility toward others for the addict because people pleasing opens the door to resentments of which we may or may not be consciously aware. This process, which results in isolating, develops gradually in some and more rapidly in others as the disease progresses. We learn different mal-adjusted coping strategies based on our false perceptions, and these are designed to make using our chemicals justified in our own minds. We don't recognize reality for what it is and refuse to learn from logical consequences.

Relying on patterns of distorted thinking explains why addicts so frequently relapse even when all of the substance has been removed from the body for a period of time. After physical withdrawal symptoms have disappeared the thinking remains. At that point we don't physically need the drug but continue our patterns of distorted thinking which isolate us from others and the real world. We react instead of rationally responding. We make poor decisions based on our excessive pride, which is our primary character defect (and what some spiritually minded people know as the first deadly sin). Our pride tells us that we should be able to make decisions for ourselves or we aren't worthy. No wonder addicts have been described as ego maniacs with inferiority complexes. Just as with this description, the addict's reactions to real events make no logical sense.

I have known several terminal addicts who insisted on using even as they were physically dying and had been advised as such by their doctor. Yet, the addict goes on using and dies in the process. Pride won't let them admit that they could be insane enough at that point to kill themselves by using. *Any rational person could see the insanity in this behavior, but at this point the addict is not sane.* Rather than admit they could be wrong in their decision to use, their pride literally kills them. The person that says they don't care really does care, *if they were in their right mind,* but they are not. Having been one who, on occasion said they wanted to die, I now recognize the insanity of trying to drink myself to death. If I had been in my right mind there are many less painful ways to kill myself and sane people don't want to die. Using insane thinking can kill, period.

Therefore, the question boils down to the basic one of "Do we want to die?" That is the reality for us mental acrobats who work without a net. (AKA addicts) The progression of the disease of substance abuse addiction will kill us unless the using is interrupted. Ideally we begin recovery, but the other interruptions that are not as much fun as recovery include confinement to a mental institution or jail (been there, and done those).

The cycle of behavior which results in negative consequences is bound to occur again if we rely on our own resources. The fact that we try to function using our distorted thinking is the problem. The solution only exists if we open our minds to reality and how to rely on help with our thinking. The argument that it can't be done is a product of distorted thinking because many of us are doing it as I write this. We are the very real evidence that it is possible to recover. We addicts are all the same in some very fundamental ways of thinking. We have all thought we were unique for some reason or another. We have to think that way to justify using after serious negative consequences. The using addict does not learn from their mistakes, but in recovery they learn a whole new way of thinking in order to enjoy living.

CHAPTER 2

The Pickle

WHEN A CUCUMBER becomes a pickle it is forever chemically altered and can never go back to being a cucumber again. It is the same way with the addict's brain, which has developed the neural connections back along the pleasure pathway that associate pleasure and what we want from substances that we take. This is not brain surgery or rocket science, it is simply reality. It is what it is. No matter how much the addict wants to be "normal" again, it is simply not going to happen. If the substance is ingested again, the connections are again pumping out the reward in the brain that keeps us coming back for more. We want to enjoy the rewards, but not suffer the side effects that happen when we use. Hell, if I could drink normally I'd get drunk every night! (Typical addictive thinking)

Because of our need to make decisions and feel good about them we have to use distorted thinking in order to rationalize that we can get what we want and get the reward but not the consequences from using. Because of my history I would have to search far and wide to find an excuse to use that I haven't tried before, but the excuse that always works in a pinch is simply I want to change the way I feel. I want the power to control the way I feel through my own actions. By taking the action to actually use I become committed to justifying my action through excuses for why I am using again.

A fancy term for the way I think after I have already started to use is called "violation of abstinence". This simply means that I get a case of "what the f—ks" because I have already done something that I told everybody I didn't want to do again. Since I already started using I might as well enjoy it and hope that I don't suffer the bad consequences. The main problem with this distorted thinking is that whenever I drink it is like a crazy surreal crap game. As it turns out it can be even worse if I drink without consequences because my denial system is reinforced and becomes stronger. I start thinking that maybe there won't be more bad consequences.

On the other hand I may get consequences as bad or even much worse than I have ever experienced. My last use of alcohol after 5 months of abstinence only lasted a few hours, but it ended up with incarceration for something I did in a blackout. So my skill at fending off consequences has weakened considerably.

I became a pickle at age 13. Today, having just turned 60 I am more like a dill than a sweet.

CHAPTER 3

The Disconnected Brain

ONE EFFECT THAT chemicals have on the brain is so closely related to the reason we create problems for the self that I feel it deserves this whole chapter.

When we ingest chemicals their effect on the brain is more than just the stimulation of the pleasure pathway. Many chemicals also shut down functions of another area of the brain, the cerebral cortex. This area acts as the filter between the primitive areas of the brain and our actions based on our primitive instincts. It is this shut-down effect that plays a major role in allowing addicts to engage in behaviors that are frowned on by our society. In other words we shut down the stop mechanism so that our feelings compel us to go, go, go.

The cerebral cortex is recognized as the conscience area of the brain. Instead of throwing up red flags of warning when we are about to do something we should know is wrong and/or downright illegal, the brain's stop mechanism is asleep. Therefore we continue to act on primitive desires and not worry about the consequences at the time. The brain becomes trained to act without the aid of the cerebral cortex over repeated using.

Relating this to my personal experience, I would never have driven drunk if I had seriously considered the consequences, but the absence of worrying about the consequences allowed me to go through with it. This was after having previous very negative consequences from doing it. Driving was simply something I wanted to do at the time, so I did it.

It is not coincidental that most people in jail were under the influence at the time they committed the crime for which they were jailed. It is a fact that criminal and addictive thinking are almost identical due to their selfish nature. (For those addicts who have not committed or been caught for a crime, please add the word "yet" to your statement of indignation.)

The after effect of our unconscionable acts is that we are then forced to rationalize and justify them based on our distorted thinking. We have to try and make them OK in our mind to make them mesh with our concept of a worthy self.

The instinctive, primitive brain is equipped to handle survival in a world where the only law is that of the jungle. Kill or be killed, eat or be eaten, take or have taken away, etc. The collective conscience of society makes it illegal to carry out primitive instincts upon others in society against their will or which could potentially harm others in society. The addict often has effectively rendered their conscience inoperable and continues to try and fulfill primitive desires. Our distorted thinking tries to rationalize that it is somehow OK. This is the reality of substance abuse addiction in civilized society. We merely get the consequences imposed by our peers for violating the rights of others to enjoy life without having to put up with our primitive acts against them.

CHAPTER 4

Working Without a Net

AS MENTIONED BEFORE there is a great desire for addicts to try to get what they want to obtain the rewards of using substances. Pride dictates that we do whatever we need to do to justify our actions. But the lure of addiction is much more powerful than just the perceived reward for me. The mystique of unpredictability of not knowing what will happen when I drink has a visceral edge that appeals to me even when I sense that I might be making a mistake.

It is the sense of going into oblivion riding the wave of euphoria with reckless abandon that has nudged me over the edge even when I thought my guard was up. When I have described this attitude to some people they often wonder if I might have a death wish. Many other addicts also experience a rush of excitement from the chaos that is created by using. From others' stories I suspect many of us have a similar desire for this type of "excitement". At least excitement is what I told myself I was looking for sometimes when I started using like there was no tomorrow. It also makes it harder to pinpoint our problems or see solutions to problems when chaos is occurring around us. "Where do we start looking when there is all this devastation?"

Creating more problems than we can cope with generates more excuses to use. "You would drink too if you had my problems." We start looking at using to forget or cover up the problems we have created. This cycle is not endless, but it usually takes confinement or death to end the cycle unless we begin recovery.

In my writing I will return again and again to my problem with pride. My fears are based on pride, and my reluctance to reach out for help is a function of pride as well. I isolate and become resentful at all my problems (most of which I have created) and my pride tells me that I should be able to cope with them. Without reaching out for the help that is available I am eliminating the potential to solve most of the problems I encounter or create for myself. I use pride to create the illusion that I am tough enough to survive anything. (After all, haven't I survived so far?) I became a martyr to myself, which is the only cause I cared about.

Eliminating the safety net of being able to reach out for help outside myself means that I am free to stew in my own coping strategy. This allows me to return to distorted thinking that eventually leads back to using. I began doing that at a fairly early age. I have explored many, many ways to rationalize why I should be able to "handle" drinking. Trying to figure the way out without help truly is like working without a net. My pride and I always try to get back to the point of thinking that maybe I can use without severe consequences.

A few years ago a girlfriend and I were binging together. She had no immediate problems except that she was facing consequences for her 3rd DUI conviction. We were both working without a net, (no outside help). Although we had both had some sober time through the miracle of AA's 12 steps, we were back operating on our own thinking. One day I laid down for a couple of hours and when I woke up she was dead.

This example is typical of the way many addicts die. We simply do not know how to self rescue, and often ignore any warning signs of imminent death that present to us. We refuse to reach out for help. Her doctor had warned her several times about the effect that alcohol and overuse of prescription drugs was having on various organ functions. She had simply refused to believe that she was going to die from doing what she liked to do; become oblivious and stimulate the pleasure pathways that had been established in her brain. With no safety net it was only a matter of when (not if) she would die. I used the event of her death extensively to justify further drinking by wallowing in self pity and guilt that I hadn't prevented her death.

CHAPTER 5

Fun Even With a Net

I F YOU HAVE had significant consequences from using and feel that using is worth the consequences because your situation is "different", welcome to the club. A feeling of uniqueness is a common trait that all addicts share. Some call it a feeling of being "apart from". Some feel superior or inferior even to other addicts. This feeling is really anything but unique if you think about the fact that it is common among addicts. Simply put, feeling unique is just a thinking distortion based on pride, and it is a major barrier to wanting a life of recovery.

All people, whether addicts or not, tend to compare themselves to others. This is not unique. It is also a fact that we have all had different life experiences. But only in addictive thinking will comparing differences kill us deader than a door nail, because this thinking will keep us from relating to other addicts that we need for their experience, strength, and hope. Yes, we can use them for their knowledge of adequate coping strategies to stay sober. In recovery it is the power of not being alone with our disease that results in the miracle of recovery.

You can take my word for it or observe it for yourself; there are recovering addicts who are not using and they actually enjoy living. If you go to meetings and still don't see it, then your perception is still distorted.

At any given point in time a recovering addict is either heading toward a relapse, or strengthening their recovery. Our odds of having a successful recovery are dramatically improved by what we can learn about life and living from others.

I will never forget my first twelve step meeting. I happened to pick a candlelight meeting and went by myself. Certain that the people were in some kind of brain washing cult, I shunned meetings and stayed miserable trying to run my own life without help for a number of years.

Why do we compare ourselves out of getting help? Our precious pride is why. Sure, some addicts stay dry without help on their own willpower, but I have never met one who acted like they enjoyed living. They always seem so up tight I don't really want my life to be like theirs anyway. I enjoy laughing at myself and uptight pride and laughing at and with others. Believe me it wasn't always like that.

I can't rely on my own thinking to stay sober. My thinking *is* my disease. The way I look at the world and interact with it is the key for enjoying life today. I can accept the fact that I need help with my distorted thinking on a daily basis. If you are getting negative consequences from substance use and think your situation is different, you are just thinking normally for an addict. That's how we justify continuing to use.

Life, for the addict, is truly what we make of it as long as we keep an open mind about accepting help. Relying on outside help let's us enjoy life instead of feeling that we are struggling to survive all the time. Life sucks when all we can do is look for the next artificial high. All of our time is spent finding excuses to use and justifying why we do it. To enjoy life and get freedom from this bondage of self we need all the help we can get.

NICHOLAS B.

Little by little at first we start becoming aware that those around us who are staying sober are doing the same thing; using the experience, strength and hope of other addicts who are staying sober. Whether they are "old-timers" who have lots of experience to draw from or "newcomers" who are desperate to learn a new way to live, we rely on others. Old-timers experience negative feelings just like everybody else; they have just learned to use effective coping strategies to deal with them. They learned these by listening to others who were staying sober and were willing to follow some simple suggestions instead of continuing to feel unique. Now they are able to pass on this knowledge which is working the 12th step of recovery: helping others. In this process we start living life on life's terms, not on our own distorted thinking terms. Living life in the real world can be very enjoyable if we accept it for what it is and learn effective coping strategies. In fact it is in doing so that frees us from the bondage of self. We can enjoy life in spite of ourselves and instead of engaging in our distorted thinking.

CHAPTER 6

The Mystery of the BIG HELP

ANYONE WHO HAS long term sobriety has the BIG HELP. You don't have to take my word for this; you can ask them about it directly. Although it is no secret, describing it is not easy. For one thing, when addicts first think about relying on a higher power, their distorted thinking works overtime to compare themselves out of wanting any help outside of self. The addict's mind is so accustomed to the idea that they are supposed to be in control of their own destiny and happiness that having faith in anything outside of their control is a scary proposition.

I must admit that my self-centered fear of not adequately describing what a higher power can mean to a recovering addict caused me concern. Then I realized that I have no power over whether someone is willing to take the leap of faith necessary to turn their life over to a power that is all encompassing. I'm not even sure about the exact moment I started trusting my higher power. I only know that it is a major miracle in my life today as it was during another period of sobriety.

My description of the how and the why of the BIG HELP is going to be inadequate not only for what it can mean to other addicts, but it remains a mystery to me as well. My sobriety today is proof enough that believing and relying on a higher power works. From listening to other addicts I know that their faith in their concept of a higher power works for them as well.

The way I look at and interact with the world is the key to my happiness. Without spending time in the dimension of the spirit I simply don't have the power to make the changes in my thinking that allow me to change the way I act.

Don't misunderstand and think I am serene all the time, I'm definitely not. I do have very serene moments when I acknowledge that things are going well without my attempts to control them. In fact, the more I don't try to control things that in reality I have no control over, things go pretty well. This fact amazes me sometimes, in spite of my pride.

It was my pride and my need to justify that my decisions were worthy even when they weren't that allowed me bulldoze through the world like it was mine and mine alone. My pride told me I didn't need help even when I did in order to be happy. The way I used to think I wouldn't have been happy *even if I had been* able to control other people. The reality of the fact that I have very little control over many things, and no control over other people kept me in constant frustration. I resorted back to the one thing I could control, my own actions based on distorted thinking. Putting a substance into my body for a reward or to become oblivious to my frustrations was easy because I thought I was in control of myself. I was wrong.

The idea that our main help comes from our journey to become more spiritual does not appeal to many addicts, who prefer to exist in their distorted thinking. It is exactly that distorted thinking that makes addiction a disease. We simply can't be happy by relying on our own thinking because our pride enters into our decisions to try to get what we want. And we will always want the selfish reward if we rely on our own thinking because the links to the pleasure pathway have been permanently established.

Any old-timer who is sober has their own concept of a Higher Power they can rely on to help make decisions. Even though there are usually growing pains, anyone, even those in early sobriety, can get a tremendous amount of relief from the fact that they don't have to try to control everything. This shifting of mental gears is called a psychic change, and can be the beginning of recovery and a happy journey through life.

Keeping an open mind will allow any addict to observe and interact with other addicts who are doing something they cannot do by themselves. I can't rely on my thinking to make me happy without consequences. I see others being happy without the consequences of using. Therefore, it is possible for me to be happy without using too. There is nothing mysterious about that type of logical thinking. It is based on something I can see for myself. It is observable data. If I choose to ignore this data I am only hurting myself.

Many addicts die each day trapped in the bondage of self without acknowledging the observable data. They would rather try to rely on their own distorted thinking than rely on a power that can't be seen without a psychic change. Being closed minded to the realm of the greatest source of power available to us is nothing but self centered pride. It also happens to be a fatal flaw in our perception of the world.

In the introduction I spoke about a six year period of sobriety. During that time I put faith in a higher power that I saw working through other people. I became convinced that putting my Son's welfare first required more than I was equipped to provide on my own. Putting someone else first was a spiritual concept. I took the leap of faith that things would work out if I did not drink and relied on a power I could not see. Eventually I stopped having gratitude for getting what we needed and started wanting more. My will, not GOD's came back into the picture.

NICHOLAS B.

The BIG HELP works often through other people, and requires an opening of a mind that has been closed by distorted thinking based on selfish pride. After all, other people exist as a result of the miracle of life too. Through listening to what sober, happy addicts have experienced in their own recoveries we discover that they are taking the necessary leap of faith. We all suffer from a disease of the spirit which did not allow for a larger view of the world than the one that our distorted thinking presented to us.

CHAPTER 7

Nothing Changes if Nothing Changes

SOMETIMES PAIN, EITHER emotional or physical, motivates change. In addiction it takes more pain in some cases than others depending on how much we are invested in our distorted thinking based on pride. People look at a down and out skid row addict and cannot imagine they are full of pride but I guarantee you they are even if you can't see it. At some point they crossed the abyss to addiction by getting the reward of using just like everyone does. Then they insisted on getting what they wanted until consequences happened. Their journey has become survival along with occasionally getting the reward of using. Every time they use they are making a choice based on pride.

The difference between a recovering addict and one who is using or heading back to relapse is the way they choose to escape the emotional pain that is created by the bondage of self. A recovering addict quits fighting the mental pain of trying to control the uncontrollable, while an addict who is using or heading for relapse chooses to fight for control. **An essential factor in this formula is that we cannot control other people.** We often get aggravated by this fact. It is what it is.

If an addict cannot find a way to accept this basic reality that we have little or no control over what other people do, he/she can get very little serenity. Just as we travel our own journey, we must let other people travel theirs.

Staying sober means a lifetime of learning this lesson over and over, in all possible scenarios.

To illustrate, think about anything that is bothering you about your life right now. Does it involve another person or people? If it gives you negative feelings, you are not only in the bondage of self; in a sense you are allowing yourself to live in the bondage of another person's actions. How does that thought make your pride feel? Those that go around acting like it doesn't bother them are simply suffering in silence, *unless they have had a psychic cha*nge. Pretending that we don't give a damn usually means that we don't have the desire to change and wish to stay in the bondage of self. We aren't flexible enough to learn new strategies for dealing with others so we hide in our inflexible shell of pretending to be tough. When we pretend to be tough, we are really hiding our fears of not being able to cope with the negative feelings generated by the fact that we have no control over others. I have gone through much of my life pretending to be tough. I thought I could handle anything life threw at me when most of the time my problems resulted from my own inability to effectively cope with negative feelings from my interactions with other people. I did not like how people acted and I reacted instead of accepting the reality that nothing I did could change their actions. In other words I set myself up to be frustrated. After enough frustration I said "the hell with it", and retreated into using. Because I enjoyed the effect, that was my strategy for many situations. I have also relapsed many times because I felt I deserved a reward if things were going well, (instead of having gratitude).

How do we get out of this rut? Sincerely having a desire to listen to others who have been through their own bondage of self and by following suggestions that worked for them is a starting point. Surrendering to the reality that we need help may not be easy on pride, but it opens up the possibility of enjoying life instead of being stuck in the bondage distorted thinking.

Continuing to rely on our own thinking without outside help does not apply a solution to the problem of being in the bondage of self. Even if we stay dry for a while on will power, it is far too easy to resort back to the thinking patterns which result in using. When we come across a plausible excuse to use, too many neural pathways in the brain lead back to the end result of rationalizing that to use is an option. Our will was hell-bent on using during the active using phase and the will does not automatically change course just because we say it has. The sub-conscious part of the brain has to be considered into the equation. Even after a period of sobriety, the fundamentally same person will use again. Distorted thoughts will eventually allow us to think that because we have purposefully stayed dry on our own, we can continue to do it without help. Without help we get back into a thinking loop that allows us to rationalize that if we use the outcome won't be so bad. "Surely the lesson has been learned", we tell ourselves. We subconsciously and then consciously start thinking we have won the battle. The reality is that the battle is never won, and the more we fight the weaker we become. The fact that we need help from others and our higher power to be happy is our reality. Any thinking not based on this reality is distorted thinking in my opinion.

NICHOLAS B.

CHAPTER 8

Physical, Mental, or Spiritual?

A DDICTION AFFECTS ALL areas of life. Our bodies become physically dependent on certain substances. Mentally we think like maniacs with a death wish. It is in the area of the spiritual that we are most deficient. We simply cannot love or even care about others in society when all we do is exist to get what we want.

It is no small wonder that most incarcerated people had problems with addiction and this played a part in why they committed crimes against others, (society). The spiritual tie-in is that we do not follow the most basic spiritual principle: The Golden Rule. How can we say we care for others when we have to feed what feels like an 800 lb. gorilla sitting on our shoulders telling us to feed it?

Yes, withdrawals from a substance can be severe, and in some cases lethal. Our thinking distortions lead us back to using even after our bodies are detoxed. Why risk inviting the gorilla to climb back on?

It is due to our lack of spirituality based on our selfish pride that leads us back to thinking we can use without the same or worse consequences. Our spiritual deficiencies are not limited to a certain type of character. People from all walks of life become addicts and fall into the bondage of self.

No, it is selfish pride, also known as the first deadly sin, which leads us down the dark path of not caring for others but only for what we want. It is spirituality, or looking at the world around us in a different way, that can lead us out of the bondage of self.

In jails and prisons respect is a big deal, but how many would have committed the crimes they were incarcerated for if they had respected their victims. It is the society of people who make the laws we live under, and somewhere under each and every crime there are victims. Many times the offender's own family becomes a victim as well if they have not already been victimized enough before the incarceration.

The bondage of self affects society in many ways no matter how much the addict preaches that they are only hurting themselves. The costs in healthcare and lost productivity alone are staggering. I won't even research the numbers because they would underestimate the actual damage created by addiction in our society. They are just part of the reality, part of the consequences that occur due to the disease of addiction. Any addict who doesn't care what he/she has to do to get the next high certainly wouldn't care about the cost to society anyway.

Another part of the spiritual sickness is the secondary denial that there is a better way to look at the world. When an addict says they can't help it they are telling the truth. Help has to come from outside their small, limited view of the world and outside their distorted thinking. Surrender and humility are the indispensible tools that can lead to change, to opening up to the possibility that they can't make good decisions based on pride.

I became stuck with the thinking that I had to figure out a way to get what I wanted. Now I have found that thinking to be the worst thing about my disease.

Like the old Rolling Stones' song I may not always get what I want, but I get what I need. Today, one of those things is guidance from a higher power that was part of me all along. After all, a higher power created me and it will only work if my pride gets out of the way.

CHAPTER 9

Another Bunch of Words for Acceptance

WHEN I WAS in my last treatment program, (hopefully), I read a book about the issues faced by members of therapeutic communities such as the one I was a member of at the time. It said that one behavioral issue that plagues addicts is that they fail to "adequately adapt their strategies when confronting negative feelings from interpersonal interaction". The reason for that, it went on, is that it allows addicts to isolate from others. When I figured out what the words meant I not only wholeheartedly agreed, but this new "insight", (or so I thought), helped me to adapt to social interactions I was having problems with at the time.

A short time later I was at a 12 step meeting where the topic was acceptance. It hit me that what the book had been describing was our topic. A basic tool in addiction recovery that is stressed so heavily in 12 step programs, acceptance is considered indispensable. I had heard the term for many years and thought I knew what it meant. However, I did not practice acceptance in my daily affairs.

Basically, the need for acceptance arises out of the fact that we have little or no control over many situations, and absolutely no control over other people. Addicts fail to adapt when interacting with others and it produces negative feelings which we react to with negative behavior. When we do not accept that things people do are out of our control we can rationalize that it is better to isolate rather than adapt. That way we are forced to rely on our own thinking which leads us back to using behavior. We may not consciously acknowledge that is what we are doing, and of course we place the blame for our negative feelings on the other person or people. That gives us plenty of excuses to justify our decision to change the way we feel with chemicals.

According to a personal story that appears in the Big Book of Alcoholics Anonymous, "Acceptance is the answer to all my problems today". Anyone who attends 12 step recovery meetings is introduced to the concept of acceptance. But few addicts are good at putting this concept into practice. We may say that we understand it. We may even preach it. But when it comes down to the reality of dealing with others whose behaviors give us negative feelings, we react to the feelings in a way that dooms us to failure. This is the equivalent of a football quarterback memorizing the playbook but never executing the plays the way they were designed. Rather than handing off the ball or passing it, he tries to run it himself on every play.

It is easy to use interactions with others to develop excuses to use. We may feel angry and build resentment toward a person in authority, for example. We may people please in order to foster resentment toward a boss who is not recognizing our efforts as much as we would like. The people we are most in contact with, our families, are an easy target for blaming. We have to isolate to think our way back to using and the family is often the biggest obstacle to doing as we selfishly please. Many addicts use a more direct approach and explode angrily toward their boss, family members, and others. The end result is the same: isolation and escape through chemical oblivion.

No matter what poor strategies we employ to isolate from others, they all can be used in our faulty rationale to escape from our feelings. Our distorted thinking allows only the options we choose, and our pride keeps us from asking for help.

Addicts new to recovery often try to focus on the negative feelings they get from someone they encounter in recovery meetings. It is no wonder because our thinking patterns are geared to isolate rather than to accept things the way they are. After all, recovery meetings are full of other sick people who have also suffered from their own distorted thinking which resulted in isolation. It is a small miracle that fights don't break out at every meeting, but they don't. We have a common purpose; that of staying sober. The end result for an addict that can't accept other people for the way they are, (even if they appear to be insufferable assholes), is that they diminish their own chance of recovery. The asshole will probably stay sober if they want recovery enough and the ones who get pissed off go out and use because of their lack of acceptance. Call it survival of the spiritually fittest. Call it reality. It happens frequently. We focus on things over which we have no control and fail to look at the important issue of staying sober. Nobody is obligated to not be an asshole. In some cases of extremely bizarre anti-social behavior a person might be banned from a meeting through a group conscience meeting of the members who call the meeting their home group. I have never seen it done unfairly or out of spite, only out of concern for the safety of the group as a whole.

Acceptance of others we would not normally care to associate with is very real and valuable training for the world outside of meetings. Sometimes a sponsor will suggest to a sponsee that he or she seek out meetings attended by people they do not like for that very reason. We are all attending because of a common disease. If we are so thin skinned that we cannot accept a fellow addict for the way they are, our chances are slim in the outside world of accepting others. Today nobody can keep me from attending whatever

NICHOLAS B.

meeting I choose, and I would certainly not consider using over such a bogus excuse. Some progress in my recovery has been made although I sometimes run across people I do not like on a personal basis. They are still fellow sufferers and I can wish for success in their recovery without liking them. (Another miracle)

CHAPTER 10

Psychic Change

PSYCHIC CHANGE IS something that is difficult to describe, like The Big Help. Some will say the two are synonymous, but others would disagree. Psychic change is something that is experiential like the serenity obtained from relying on the Big Help. Most times it is gradual, but it can also happen in a short time. It is observable by both the one experiencing it and by others observing the behavior of the person it has happened to.

The fact that psychic change can and does occur on a regular basis would seem to make the disease of substance addiction seem fairly tame compared to other fatal diseases. Having a treatment option that works gives the diseased person an opportunity to lead a productive life *once the psychic change has taken place*.

Because the problem that creates the diseased state within the person is as much spiritual as biological, the affected person does not always willingly go along with actions that allow the psychic change to take place. This means that relatively few addicts are willing to ask for needed help or accept it when it is offered. As Einstein once stated "the consciousness that created the problem cannot be the one solving it".

The basis for a psychic change seems to be the willingness of the addict to give up one's own distorted thinking, hence the need to seek help outside of one's own thinking. Distorted thinking is a primary component (symptom) of the disease of addiction. The best the sufferer can do is trust that what others who are successfully recovering say works for them. Once this leap of faith is made it opens up the mind sufficiently to allow for personal recovery and growth.

Most people who experience psychic change realize they have gone through it after the fact. By following suggestions they wouldn't have thought of doing on their own, their change in behavior somehow leads to a change in thinking. This further reinforces the fact that outside help is essential to recovery. When the recovering addict discovers that they no longer obsess about using, and that experiencing real life is preferable to the consequences derived from using, they are suddenly on the right track. The trick at this point is realizing that their addictive thinking was distorted, that relying on other resources makes life better, not worse, and that they need to continually do this in order to stay sober. A person who has experienced a psychic change does not think about the process as work, but as dealing with *life on life's terms*. (Also known as reality)

The key to continued growth rests in the quality of spiritual growth, or spiritual journey that the addict pursues. The danger in not undertaking this journey is that pride can lead the addict into distorted thinking that they helped themselves rather than the reality that they allowed themselves to be helped. Everyone needs some alone time, and at these times a higher power of the addict's own concept is needed to remind us that our distorted thinking is still around. Praying, meditating, chanting, or other forms of communication with this power of the addict's own choosing will help the addict make decisions based on reality rather than distorted thinking.

At an early age we seem to be instinctively aware of reality; that we are not in control. We may not like it but it is our reality. Through the magic of chemicals we begin our distorted thinking journey and try to control based on what we think we want. Instead of sticking with reality, we begin to imagine that we can have what we want instead of being grateful for getting what we need. Reality goes out the window. As consequences which should bring us back to reality begin to occur, our pride results in more distorted thinking that we have to justify our actions. Even as we slip deeper into the insanity of addiction, our pride keeps us defending our actions. Throw in the physical craving that is real when we begin to withdraw from a substance, and our distorted thinking leads us progressively down the tubes.

That is why I think, (because others told me so), the change has to occur at the spiritual level. Science has not yet devised a way to cause someone to want to get sober. "How many psychiatrists does it take to change a light bulb? Only one, but the light bulb has to *want* to change."

It is unfortunate that people are literally dying every day to provide evidence of the killing power of pride. It is also a fact the many are having a psychic change every day and beginning their recovery journey. Keeping an open mind will make us realize that anyone can do it if they really want to. Only the bondage of self can keep the door to recovery locked.

NICHOLAS B.

CHAPTER 11

Paradoxes

A S IN ALL journeys in life, the road to recovery has apparent paradoxes. The fact that this word exists tells me that addicts are probably not the only ones who spend time pondering their meaning. The most obvious is the concept that in addiction we must "give up to win". Addicts will use a paradox such as this to find an excuse to stay out of recovery. After all, doesn't society tell us that giving up is a bad thing to do? But like other thinking distortions, finding reasons to stay out of recovery is part of our diseased thinking process. For those lucky enough to have gone through the psychic change and stay in recovery mode, the apparent paradoxes are not a legitimate reason to leave recovery. For myself, I know now that "I must not give up on trying to give up my distorted thinking in order to win".

Let's take the paradox of the necessity to give up our thinking to win. We can't rely on our own thinking based on pride and what we want. Our actions based on thinking this way will result in more negative consequences. By giving up our prideful, selfish thinking that we can control things out of our control, we are actually getting control of our disease. That is the reality of the way recovery works. The Big Book of Alcoholics Anonymous says that lack of power *is* our dilemma, and that is so very true. We haven't got the power to fix ourselves, therefore the power must come from an outside source.

I have heard it said that an addict is like a punch drunk boxer who keeps agreeing to fight, knowing deep down that he cannot win. He keeps stepping into the ring and getting beat up. Since this is all he knows, he never considers the option of not getting into the ring in the first place. If he did not get into the ring he would not get beat up again. He keeps thinking he can win, and his thinking is not based on the reality of the situation. In the rooms of 12 step recovery programs people often say "my best thinking got me here". To me that statement is also a paradox. Our thinking created the reason we need to seek recovery in 12 step meeting rooms, and the fact that we finally accept our disease and recognize that we can actually get some relief from the bondage of self in these rooms keeps us coming back. Those of us who do finally get into the rooms of recovery are the lucky ones.

Another thinking paradox is that addicts from all different backgrounds need the same process to recover. Addicts have all thought they were different, but this is not the reality when it comes to our thinking. We have all had distorted thinking that kept us in the denial of our disease and denial that recovery would work for us. We all think our situations are different, and they may be in some particulars. Yet when it comes to our self-centered thinking based on false and misplaced pride, we are all the same. We use whatever situation is at hand to think our way back to using. If we don't hear things in meetings we can relate to, we aren't listening or haven't been to enough meetings.

When I first started going to 12 step meetings a lot of little things people did or said pissed me off. Now nothing a person does or says at a meeting could keep me out. My old way of thinking was to look for things to be upset about. Now I realize that I have no control over what people do or say regardless of whether I agree with it or not. Paradoxes or differences in individual stories no longer have the power to make me want to compare or think my way out of recovery.

NICHOLAS B.

CHAPTER 12

Going With the Flow

A DDICTS CREATE CHAOS in their lives in order to justify using behavior. We have a hard time being told what to do or what not to do because it threatens our false sense of pride that we cultivate about our ability to make decisions. These decisions about what we do are based on false pride because they are selfish and self-centered. We make decisions that eventually make using a justifiable option in our diseased minds.

Not being adaptable in our way of dealing with different situations involving other people is a good example of going against the flow to create chaos. As the disease process progresses we learn to react to others in ways that will generate negative feelings in almost any situation. For example rather than calmly responding when angered, we might fly into tantrums rather than asserting ourselves appropriately. Worse, we might stuff our feelings into the sub-conscience and later turn them into resentments. The conflicts that arise in the mind of an addict are generated without much thought that we plan to turn our negative feelings into excuses to use later.

Addicts tend to approach interpersonal interactions with a win-lose attitude because of our pride. Since effective interpersonal interaction requires give and take, our win-lose attitude is more likely to generate negative feelings. Then we have reasons to isolate from others that we blame for these feelings.

After accumulating the garbage in our sub-conscious mind from not dealing with negative feelings adequately, we have the ammunition we need to feel justified in using a chemical to feel better. We learn to celebrate victories based on false pride, and mourn losses for the same reason. Either way gives us an excuse to use. The fact that these imagined battles are only going on in our diseased mind makes our self destructive behavior seem bizarre to other people. Our rationalizations to use make perfect sense to us, just not to the real world.

The flow of life is largely out of our control, save the way we respond. Our false pride tells us we must try to win instead of negotiating, and this thinking is not based in reality. Once we want to stay sober we learn that in most situations we can go with the flow or negotiate rather than generating negative feelings by trying to buck the current of reality. Today when I catch myself doing this I can usually laugh and apologize for my self-centered reactions. To simply ignore them is to invite conflict in my magnificent magnifying mind.

Most of us have been bucking the current for quite a while in order to always have a negative feeling handy to bring up as an excuse. The Big Book of Alcoholics Anonymous says that we "will not regret the past nor wish to shut the door on it". It also says we must "cease fighting anything or anybody" and that "resentment is the number one offender" that we use to justify using.

Life itself brings challenges, mostly involving how we respond to other people. Like rapids on a river that have to be negotiated in order to continue on our journey we have to negotiate with others to live effectively. Trying to paddle back upstream is not only a bitch, but it gets us nowhere. Trying to apply win-lose criteria to our interpersonal interactions is not an effective technique to successfully continue our life journey without getting stuck on self-made obstacles. Life itself will provide all the excitement we can handle.

NICHOLAS B.

CHAPTER 13

The Real Adventure

THE REASON ADDICTS get stuck in the lifestyle of using is because it becomes all we know how to do. In our distorted thinking we think that we are in control of our feelings, but the reality is that our feelings are controlling us. By staying stuck in this mode we fail to fulfill needs and have no chance to think about ourselves as worthy, (we can't self-actualize). We are not necessarily bad people; we are sick people who have learned to deal with life inappropriately. As a by-product we do not respect the life given to us, let alone the lives of others who stand to get in the way of what we think we want.

During this process, we do not live in the reality of life. We progress into a seemingly hopeless state of mind. I say seemingly because by making it seem hopeless in our mind we have still more excuses to use to feel better. The reality is that real life is right around the corner as soon as we surrender instead of trying to fight and control. When we quit using the real adventure begins. The amazing thing is that we don't have to do it alone. In fact, we can't do it alone and be happy.

As I write this millions of people as seemingly hopeless as I thought I was are enjoying real life. It's like living life over, because I had forgotten what it was like to live in reality. Since my brain remembers the reward of using, I can't rely on my willpower to guide me. Most of life happens and I accept it. When I can't intuitively make a decision I ask for guidance from my own concept of a higher power. For reasons I went over in Chapter 5, I won't go into my personal concept of a higher power, but it is working for me today.

What is really amazing to me is that the things I do today are fun and rewarding because I don't always do everything selfishly. I have the opportunity to be selfish if I want to but I can actually enjoy sharing and learning with others. I used to think I was some kind of rugged individualist who would enjoy "surviving" on my own. I almost died that way.

The real adventure is the adventure of living life on life's terms. After all, I didn't do a very good job doing it on mine. Teaching a 6 year old basic sports skills or how to type on a computer may not sound like a real adventure, but don't knock it if you haven't tried it. Believe me, it is an adventure. Better yet, try to get her to be quiet in the woods so we can see more deer. Now that is a challenge.

Many recovering addicts are helping others to realize that living life on life's terms is not only possible, it's preferable. When working the steps of recovery, we not only get a reward out of helping others, we are doing the right thing. Plus, we are not dwelling on our own selfish desires when we do this. It takes us out of the bondage of self.

Pitfalls in recovery are as close as the next time we interact with another person and come away with negative feelings. We cannot control the fact that we get the negative feelings, only how we will respond to them. When thought about that way life is all about the adventure of avoiding the pitfalls once we begin the recovery process. Since our previous reactions to negative feelings were bringing bad consequences, the process to adequately adapt to them is of paramount importance. It is literally a matter of life and death for addicts. And that makes life an adventure for me. If this process is

NICHOLAS B.

not a priority I begin walking on a slippery slope back toward relapse. The thought of taking a drink of alcohol today literally makes me sick to my stomach, just as drinking dreams do occasionally. Drinking thoughts and dreams do occur as a part of the sub-conscious thought process, but they do not lead to the nightmare of using anymore.

CHAPTER 14

Some Are Sicker Than Others

SOME ADDICTS HAVE ravaged their bodies with using. Some have co-occurring mental and/or medical problems which present challenges that I cannot address in this writing due to lack of knowledge. In fact, I have found that the more I learn, the more I don't know. But this book deals with the thinking that keeps addicts like me in the bondage of self. From observing others who have mental and medical problems other than addiction, it appears that there is little hope of addressing other problems unless the addiction problem is dealt with first.

For one thing, our self prescribed substances change the effect of any legitimate medications. Sometimes the combination can be deadly. But at the very least our drugs of choice often alter any beneficial effect other drugs prescribed to treat a co-occurring condition may have. Many find that sobriety itself allows us to eventually forego other prescribed medications while others find that needed medications are finally allowed to fully do their job.

In some co-occurring cases of mental illness, the same treatment to treat addiction also treats the other mental illness as well. Knowing that it is our thinking that precipitates the problem, the willingness to give up our distorted thinking can do wonders for many conditions. Paramount to this is the willingness to reach out for help. Help from others and from our higher power of choice can only work if we ask for it and allow it to. There is one major difference from "getting it all out" with a psychiatrist and sharing with a sponsor and at meetings. Psychiatrists have to be paid, and meetings and sponsors are free. Meetings usually take up a donation to pay for expenses like coffee but the donation is not mandatory.

When it comes to addiction the measure of how sick we are is the extent we are unwilling to reach out for help and how much we are unwilling to accept it. The fact is that all the help we need is available to us, but it doesn't do a bit of good if we don't accept it. Pride is the primary defect we all share that gets in the way of recovery.

All addicts die with their disease. We have all been pickled. If we are lucky we don't have to die from it. When I say this I'm not talking about any irreversible damage we've done to our bodies. I'm talking about going to the grave with the false pride-based idea we are in control right to the end.

That is the way most addicts die. We keep our stubborn pride and insist on using until it kills us. Whether while driving head-on into another car in a blackout, getting shot in a police standoff, getting a hot shot shooting up, drowning in our own vomit, or shutting down our organs. We keep on thinking it can't happen to us until it finally does. Even if we acknowledge that it can happen to us, we do it anyway because we want to be in control of the way we feel. Pride is pride; it's false and misplaced in all addicts. All the other stuff just serves to confuse the real issue.

I've seen it happen and said I didn't care if it happened to me. All of life is a gamble, right? By some miracle composed of enough consequences, divine intervention, and gratitude I don't want to go out that way today.

I have known for a number of years that I didn't have to die while on a bender, but I don't think about it if I take the first drink. That is because my distorted thinking leads me to take the first one and it gets even more distorted when I artificially stimulate my pleasure pathway. Then I literally have no choice in the matter and have no control of using still more. Trying to use in a controlled manner is so frustrating to me that it's just not worth the effort. That is fighting, and I did that my whole addicted life. It is the opposite of what I have to do to treat my disease.

My old thinking comes and goes, and I haven't had to act on it lately. I give up my will each day to a power I can't describe or understand. I would like to take credit for my sobriety because that is my nature. If I did take credit for it I would be in trouble and mistakenly think I was in control. I'm just not as sick as I used to be. I try to have progress, not perfection. Recovery is a process of being aware of distorted thinking and acknowledging it for what it is. It is not a cure, just treatment on a daily basis. Some days are better than others just like some of us are sicker than others. The more I'm willing to surrender to the fact that my distorted thinking is not based in reality, the less sick I am. I can live with that.

NICHOLAS B.

CHAPTER 15

Progress, Not Perfection

HAVING UNATTAINABLE GOALS is easy when you always want more of anything you think you want. Addicts take full advantage of this thinking distortion to give up on recovery and return to the cycle of addictive thinking. Left to our own thinking we pick and choose things as goals that result in negative feeling when they can't be achieved. I personally made that mistake by trying to "will" myself into serenity after I had experienced this feeling. I simply didn't have the power. The power had to come from outside myself.

Many addicts say they want to "get" recovery, then have a let down when it doesn't happen the way they want it to. I've seen people go to the recommended 90 meetings in 90 days, then get high because they aren't "cured". There is no cure for addictive thinking. We are making progress if we recognize distorted thinking when we have it. It beats the hell out of following through on it and actually using.

Again, you don't lose addictive thinking by will power, but luckily it is recognizable if we look for it. It is simple really. If something is out of our control and it upsets us, it's addictive thinking. We might not be able to do anything about it, but we can talk and pray about it. Somehow in the talking and the praying, along with acceptance, we don't have to use over it. If we do it's on us and a result of our will which is always based on pride.

The addict selects things to try to be perfect at that are impossible to achieve to give them an excuse for negative feelings. Since these are things out of our control, getting upset about them is distorted thinking as a result of the disease. Of course most addicts could be called compulsive, and we all suffer from the mental illness part of addiction. We select what to obsess over even if we do it sub-consciously.

The process of learning to recognize distorted thinking is a process that is on-going. New situations and opportunities to become frustrated because of our very real powerlessness occur as a natural part of living. But it is really not all that hard to identify distorted thinking in action. Negative feelings based on our dealings with other people will continue to happen and will interrupt our serenity. It is when we quit fighting and suppressing these feelings, acknowledge our powerlessness, and ask for help with them that we improve in living life on life's terms. Getting upset over things we have no control over is part of who we are. Learning to accept situations is part of who we want to become *if* we want to stay sober. Thinking that we could become perfect at doing this is a function of false pride.

NICHOLAS B.

CHAPTER 16

A Word on Religion

ALTHOUGH MY OLD Pappy never cautioned me about avoiding discussion about religion or politics I've learned that lesson over the years. Because I have personally seen the topic of religion be used as an excuse to avoid recovery, I'm going to mention it. Obviously this sets me up for criticism from anyone who doesn't agree with me, but so does writing this book.

My recovery is dependent on a higher power, I'm certain of that. On my own will I would destroy myself. Although my feelings fluctuate almost on a daily basis about the best method to interact and ask for help from this creative force, the only thing I need be concerned with is that the power is there for me to call on. All religions have the same problem with credibility in my opinion. The interpretations are handled by mere mortals like me.

I do know that addicts hate having things shoved down their throat by others and sometimes I feel that way when I go to church, but not always. I also know that my lack of acceptance of others and what they profess to believe can be a major problem. I cannot control others. I never have been able; I never will be able to. Therefore, accepting that others believe in their own minds what they say is a big improvement over wanting to argue details. The spiritual spark that ignited my belief that I could live in recovery began by listening to others describe their own recovery and how they cope with problems in life.

Among the things I have seen in recovery are addicts that will not attend recovery meetings because of the mention of GOD. It is a very easy excuse because the recovery steps most readily available and which have been used by millions use the word GOD. Addicts new to recovery and those ready to use again will look for any excuse to become indignant and compare themselves out. I guess hearing the word GOD works as well as any other excuse for those who are not willing to reach out for help.

Those who allow what others say about GOD and personal beliefs to build into resentment that they can use as an excuse are merely suffering from pride. After all, at the core of the disease of addiction is the need to isolate and dwell in our own distorted thinking, and what better excuse is there than to let what others do or say in meetings annoy us? Basically what such a person is thinking is that they know better than someone else about the unexplainable force that drives the universe.

The Big Book of Alcoholics Anonymous suggests treating such a person as if they were a spiritually sick friend. Whether they get over their spiritual sickness before it kills them is out of our control. The worst thing we could do is let someone else make us spiritually sick too.

Today I feel that the vehicle used to relate to a higher power is not as important as recognizing there is one. Any religion is a good one for the addict if that concept works, and many use 12 step recovery meetings as "church". Most of us tried to be our own higher power even if we were brought up with a religious background. And trying to be our own higher power is the thinking distortion that keeps us in the disease of addiction.

Once the spark is ignited and we really want to stay sober, there is nothing anyone else can do to make us relapse. No one is going to pour a drink

NICHOLAS B.

down my throat. I heard an Episcopal Priest speak at an AA convention once that put it in perspective for me. He said that he went to church to save his soul and AA to save his ass. He also said that church was for people who didn't want to go to hell and AA was for people who had been there and didn't want to go back. I also knew an avowed atheist who used the collective gathering at meetings as his higher power. (Group of Drunks = GOD, or if you prefer, Group of Druggies)

I don't want to use today. No one can make me but I could easily make myself if I start manufacturing negative feelings based on what other people say or do. Getting upset about what others use for their own higher power is just not worth it.

CHAPTER 17

Every Day Is Training Day

"MY WORST DAY sober was better than my best day using". That may sound like a cliché, but it is the truth. Not that I didn't have days I thought were really fun, especially where sex and women were concerned, but the fun using days reinforced my diseased thinking process. They helped set me up for the big fall from negative consequences. Most negative consequences were summarily dismissed or minimized in my mind with the hope that the next using experience would be different. We addicts are great at selectively remembering the reward of using and forgetting the negative consequences.

I guess you could say that I agree with a behaviorist philosophy that holds that actions are based on learned patterns of behaviors designed to achieve rewards. Normally, negative consequences will extinguish undesirable behavior because of the lack of reward. With substance addiction the reward happens in the pleasure pathway of the brain almost every time we use. To rationalize using addicts use distorted thinking to minimize negative consequences.

What are the rewards of not using? The obvious is not creating further negative consequences. Even more important is the serenity of living life on life's terms and the spiritual payoff of not feeing like such a shithead all the time. By treating others in a compassionate, caring way we learn to get the reward of being a part of the human race without doing more harm than good. Why should we even care about the rest of the human race? Because deep down we want others to care about us and it's the right thing to do. Doing the right things gives us a peace of mind that cannot be achieved by living selfish lives.

At any rate, how is this possible? We do this by a willingness to learn new coping strategies for the realities of life. The details of how to do this are available at your local 12 step meeting from others in recovery.

I know the principle involved in order to learn a wrestling move well enough to make it work in a match. The principle is this: It is not enough to know how to work a move. You have to practice the move until it becomes "bulletproof" and you do it without even thinking about it. You practice it in all situations, and with many different partners. You work the move over and over in your mind, even while getting ready to go to sleep. When you wake up you think about using it on the first person you see. You become invested in the move. The move becomes a part of you. It is simply something you do.

This same principle applies to recovery. We used to be invested in finding ways to use and justifying why it was OK. We reinforced using behavior until it happened without even thinking about it, and the consequences were a bitch. New moves have to be learned to override the old behavior. We can escape the bondage of self by practicing principles of recovery until they are automatic. We have to apply the principles in all situations. We have help and using that help is part of the move. We used to have excuses. Not anymore. Like the psychiatrist's light bulb, we have to want to change.

Recovery is not about using help once to release us from the bondage of self. We are too close to the problem; we need help every day. Today was another training day. Tomorrow will be too. Making every day a training day beats the hell out of the alternative, which would keep me in the bondage of self, and bring more negative consequences.

NICHOLAS B.

CHAPTER 18

Simple Answer, Complicated Lives

K EEP IT SIMPLE, easy does it, one day at a time, let go and let God, etc. These are all slogans used in 12 step recovery, and they are used to remind us that the process of recovery does not have to be all that complicated *if* we can do these things *all* the time. There lies the rub. We learn as we move on to new situations or encountering old situations without our substances that old thinking patterns are still present in our hard wiring.

We cannot be perfect and not act on feelings all the time. Thinking back now I can see how I acted on my own will to use and get into trouble and made any real or imagined problems worse. Hindsight, as they say, is 20/20.

But what about in the future? If we are not aware of the need to accept our powerlessness in each situation that calls for it, are we doomed? The answer is a thousand times *NO*! Progress, not perfection, remember?

Like the journey of life itself, recovery is full of variables for each of us that make each journey different. Recovery is about reaching out to the available help. Help in the form of discussing feelings and problems with others in recovery. And even bigger help is available from our concept of a higher power, (the Big Help).

BUT, and this is a big BUT, the extent that addicts use the help available also varies widely. Some of us let the Big Help guide us directly, and others rely more on this help by interacting more with others. Some like the fellowship of the group meetings, and some rely more heavily on a sponsor to guide them. Some stress the importance of following the 12 steps to the letter in a structured manner, and others seek to intuitively take right actions through constant reliance on their higher power. Some get more out of their personal inventory to identify how their pride and other character defects affected their past actions and others get more out of making direct amends to those who we they harmed in the past.

I cannot judge what is needed by other individuals. I do know that we can go through life without using because I see people every day that are doing it. They have been freed from the bondage of self enough to stay sober.

All I can do is acknowledge the evidence before me. As the Big Book of Alcoholics Anonymous says, "It works, it really does". If I were to disagree, I would be engaging in distorted thinking for not believing the evidence I see with my own eyes. And I can guarantee you that I am doing it with help by trying to give up my will and not by using my willpower. Today, and just for today, I will stay sober. I have a good chance of doing it again tomorrow if I am willing to accept help. By accepting help I am freed from the bondage of self. It really is that simple.

NICHOLAS B.

CHAPTER 19

The Wheels Will Fall Off

THE HUMAN EXPERIENCE insures that at some point life will cause us pain and suffering. I have often wondered if failure to accept our own mortality is one of the reasons addicts self destruct. Maybe our self centered pride tells us it is better to try and have a hand in controlling how we are going to end our own existence.

The point is that we are going to have problems of one sort or another, and finally die. My selfish pride tells me I may as well go out oblivious to it all, not caring how it affects others.

Realizing how hard I made it for others and myself somehow makes me want to at least have a better quality of life than I could get on my own. This awareness that is part of my spiritual experience is something I could not have imparted to myself. Therefore it came from something outside of me. I can only hope, (and pray), that the next time the wheels fall off I'm reaching out for help instead of trying to fix it myself.

Using the wheels falling off example reminds me of the state my mind can get in when I drink. One of my DUIs resulted in me hitting a light pole after failing to negotiate a turn. I was in a blackout at the time, but talked to the Cop who arrested me a few days later. He said that when he got to the scene I was walking around my car and repeatedly kicking the tires and cussing at the car, as if it were the car's fault that it had hit the light pole.

That was the way I lived my life most of the time. I would take actions based on my diseased thinking and try to blame the results on someone or something else. Referring back to the Einstein quote in a previous chapter; "if I am the creator of the problem, my consciousness cannot solve the problem". I should have never considered driving that night as on innumerable others but I insisted on it. The thought that there might be a problem never occurred in my consciousness.

How do we cope when the wheels fall off? My pride tells me to fix it myself. But today I know the first thing to do is talk to someone who knows about wheels and let them share with me their experience in the matter. Most of life's legitimate problems I have little control over. Most of my perceived problems stem from my interactions with other people and the feelings I get from that. I can't control my initial feelings, and today I am aware of that fact. The BIG HELP is always there waiting for me to surrender and ask for help. My reactions don't result in harm to myself and others like they used to. Then things often work out the way they are supposed to without interference from me. Again, it often amazes me how that process works when I stay out of it.

NICHOLAS B.

CHAPTER 20

Bridges Across

T HE BRIDGE THAT I would like to build to go back across the abyss of addiction will never be built. I have been altered by my disease and will be plagued by my need to control and the thought that I could use a chemical to change my feelings for the rest of my life. Because of the bridges that have been built by others and a higher power, I can cross the other abyss' I encounter today. I will not be perfect and may not instinctively know that I am powerless in every situation and not think about controlling something about it. I do know that when I get aggravated at others I am not surrendering to my powerlessness to control and it's time to reach out for help.

Having awareness that my feelings are often a product of distorted thinking is the result of what others have discovered. I have to rely on help from outside of me to show me what the reality is. Similar to using a spell checker to check what the plural of abyss is, I rely on outside help to guide me in my powerlessness and to decide if any action would be appropriate. Many times the answer is to do nothing. I can be comfortable with that option today.

That is the good news. As they say, "to be aware is to be alive". Sometimes I notice a detail of living and it is like experiencing it as a child. Loving someone unconditionally, noticing a detail in nature, making amends after reacting in anger, and going through the day with gratitude are things that can give me such a feeling of joy that I want others to experience it too. The bad news, if any, is that I cannot do these things all the time. Giving up my attempt to control is progress for me. When I have a negative feeling today I usually get uncomfortable enough that I realize there is something I am not accepting and want to control. Awareness in this light beats the hell out of the alternative of making myself miserable. I can accept the answer even though I don't always have to like it much. It's just not worth my sobriety or sanity to dwell on something I can't control. Such feelings used to control me. Now they don't have that power.

Not reacting to negative feelings and accepting situations for what they are does not bother me like it used to. I hope that it means that I am making progress but I guarantee this is not a technique that comes to me easily. My pride tells me to handle things myself and not discuss them with my peers in meetings or with someone in private. I have found that I can usually surrender to my concept of a higher power in any surrounding. This is also something that does not come naturally to an addict who used to spend enormous amounts of time rationalizing in order to find an excuse to use. I spent a lot of time commiserating about problems that came up. I used to say "poor me, pour me another one".

I do not afford myself the luxury of dwelling on the one abyss I cannot go back across. Bridges of recovery provide me the opportunity to cross the abyss' ahead, not wistfully want to go back. For all I know it might have been my higher power's plan all along for me to suffer so I would seek to open communication and to try to understand GOD's will for me. To shut the door on past mistakes would invite not being able to learn from them. While I was physically imprisoned I became familiar with a workbook entitled *The Key to Your Expected End*. Just when I got to a part in the

NICHOLAS B.

workbook that said we could pray to have our captivity shortened, lo and behold they changed my release date, and I got out earlier than expected. And yes, I had been praying for that. Although I'm not sure whether that could be called a spiritual experience, it definitely reinforced my belief in the power of prayer.

CHAPTER 21

The Most Sober Man I Know

I CONSIDER MYSELF to be very fortunate indeed to know and love Dan C., who is also the most sober man I know. He began his sobriety journey the year I was born, which means that as of this writing he is 60 years sober.

It is a local tradition in my area to celebrate Dan's sobriety anniversary with a big potluck dinner and speaker. Dan is aware that help from his higher power is what is keeping him sober. He would be the first to acknowledge that the promise he made to surrender his will, and the fact that he has managed to do just that on a daily basis, is the reason he is sober.

You see, Dan has taken the most important step and worked it perfectly for those 60 years. He knows down to his core he is powerless over alcohol, and has learned to accept that certain things in life are out of his control. The pain he still occasionally feels by not accepting the reality of some situations allows him to grow rather than wilt from the experience.

The meeting he says he has gotten the most out of is a "step" meeting which reviews the 12 steps of AA on a continual basis. This serves to remind him that the basic principles of living with addiction and staying sober have not changed in 60 years. In fact, these principles have been around longer than Alcoholics Anonymous. Dan also believes that the steps work for addictions other than alcohol and is not hung up like some people on a singleness of purpose in AA. Dan has seen the devastation of addictions other than alcohol first hand over the years.

Dan enjoys going to meetings, and now in his 90s he still continues to sponsor and help others in recovery. Hearing the trials and tribulations of those of us who still struggle with the bondage of self also reminds him that the same "character defects" which plague us from the time we cross into addiction are the same ones he still encounters.

I think that Dan would agree with me that the chief problem with addicts is pride, which leads to a lack of acceptance of reality. When he describes this lack of acceptance he says "you have to take it from up here (pointing to his head), to here" (pointing to his chest). My interpretation is that we have to get it into our subconscious thought. We have to internalize acceptance until it is a part of who we are. My philosophy contained in Chapter 17: Every Day Is Training Day represents the influence Dan has made on me in my sobriety journey.

It's not that Dan doesn't ever get aggravated; it is that he recognizes what causes his frustration. Pride, which is at the root of all our character defects, still occasionally bothers this man with 60 years of sobriety. It never goes away entirely so the process of recovery must continue on a daily basis even for him. It would be ignorant for me to suppose that it might magically disappear in my life. Even thinking that it ought to go away entirely is distorted thinking based on pride.

CHAPTER 22

Gotta Want To Want It

DESIRE TO STAY sober does not come easily for addicts. I know that sounds like repeating the obvious, but it is a reality that bears repeating. Just because we say we want to stay sober doesn't mean a lot when we have spent the majority of our addicted lives lying to ourselves and others about our intentions.

When our thinking *is* the disease the ability to elevate to living a spiritual life is mandatory. The desire to do the right things, even if they cause pain to our pride is the equivalent of crossing another abyss. The difference this time is that there is a well constructed bridge. Because the bridge is well constructed by others, it does not have to be difficult to cross. Help is there every step of the way if we reach out for it.

On the other hand, because the bridge remains over this abyss, we can cross back over and start relying on our own will fairly easily. Most addicts relapse and do not get it right the first time. Our whole existence has evolved around what we want, and doing things in our own way. The fact that we wanted oblivion instead of reality and that our actions have been fueled by our distorted thinking based on false and misplaced pride can be too big of a pill (no pun intended), for many of us to swallow. Again, this is the reality. Addiction is a disease of relapse. It doesn't have to be, but for the majority of addicts who try to get sober, it happens. We have a hard time entering into and staying in the spiritual dimension that brings about psychic change.

I guess one way I measure progress is the amount of awareness about my negative feelings I have. It is essential to be aware of negative feelings toward others and things I cannot control. This is where the spiritual being comes alive inside of me. Now that I know what causes the negative feeling, the sooner I reach out for help, the less emotional pain I have to experience. Nor can I force myself to give up my will. After all, forcing anything is the opposite of surrendering. Accepting the powerlessness I truly have about the actions of others is something I will need help with for the rest of my life.

Like I said earlier in this writing I have a chance if I stay in training each day. I have to assume I will never understand my concept of GOD because the concept keeps expanding. I see it mostly on a day to day basis through others.

Today I can have gratitude to feel the emotional pain of being wrong and unable to control so many things, instead of the oblivion of feeling nothing at all. In order for life to be enjoyable I have to actually live it instead of running away from all the realities. If I cross back over the spiritual bridge and start relying on my will I will have to do it alone. I will have to start thinking again that I can do it alone. Then I will be back to relying on my own diseased, distorted thinking. I have learned from experience that life doesn't get better when I do this, only worse.

Today, and just for today I want to want sobriety. I have no argument with reality today. Today I understand that my feelings can come and go like the wind, but reality is constant and recognizable for what it is. I can even handle it with help.

CHAPTER 23

Joy

MOST ADDICTS WHO are living in recovery for a period of time do so for the rewards that become more important than the bogus rewards of using. One of these rewards is a feeling that can only be described as joy. This feeling, I think, arises out of awareness that we can actually enjoy life in the absence of trying to control everything around us. This includes not having to center our lives on the use a chemical which is only a part of a great relief from the bondage of self.

We, who have gone through our addicted lives based on what we thought we wanted and not knowing that our thinking was flawed start becoming comfortable with the fact that living life on life's terms can bring us joy. We can accept that other people's actions are out of our control just as much as the forces in nature. We can control other people no more than we can control the sun, rain, or wind. We have our place as a part of the whole, not the master of it. We have learned the consequences from trying to play GOD. Our old perception of the world was fatally flawed.

Our lives have been the equivalent of a young child who, full of joy in a meadow chasing butterflies, suddenly catches one. The end of the butterfly's flight also ends the joy of the chase. The joy was in the chase, not what the child thought it wanted. The consequence is the end of the chase.

The addict chases the feeling of euphoria, which in reality brings disastrous consequences. Experiencing the journey of life with acceptance without having to control is what brings us joy. Spirituality is not waiting for a miracle to happen to us, it is recognizing the miracles that exist all around us.

We cannot force this feeling of joy; it comes through surrender to reality. There is nothing wrong with living life; we can do so with vigor. With relief from the bondage of self we can explore all that life has to offer including joy. It is impossible to experience joy without also experiencing the natural pains of living. Emotional pain and joy are the yin and yang of life. Without experiencing one there is nothing to compare the other to. Without the joy that living a more spiritual life brings, the addict sees no reason to change and will go back to using. Emotional pain comes as a result of lack of acceptance of the realities in life. *Joy comes as a result of giving up trying to control the uncontrollable.* That is the simple reality of life for the addict.

Other people can be caught up in the bondage of self but their consequences are not usually as harsh as ours. Many of us have significant others or family members who want to control us. The bondage of self is not limited to addicts, but the bondage of self in addiction makes addiction a fatal disease. It is a good bet that those who try to control us, (even if we are in recovery), will experience no joy from their efforts, and we may feel they are a real pain in the ass. But accepting them as they are will keep us from using them as an excuse to use chemicals.

CHAPTER 24

Nobody Said Simple Was Easy or Life Was Fair

ONE THING THAT many addicts get confused about is the difference between the words simple and easy. I would like to say that when I am in my right mind and things are going my way, recovery seems easy. Simply recognizing when I am not accepting things I have no control over can't be that hard, right? I mean that sounds like a pretty simple concept.

How easily we forget that our whole existence as addicts revolved around trying to control to get what we wanted along with a need to be right about our decisions. How could we be that wrong about something that important?

Addicts in recovery often have an urge to complicate the simple. Some addicts never have to relapse. Some never recover from the endless cycle of trying to prove that they can be in control of things they have no control over.

A major breakthrough in spiritual growth is realizing that other people deserve the same consideration that we expect even if we feel we are treated unfairly. The Golden Rule principle applies in order to live a spiritual life. We would not want others to treat us the way we have treated them with our selfish motives.

The thought of surrendering makes us shudder and want to move on to another subject. The fact that it is surrendering to reality does little to ease our misery at the prospect that we could be so wrong. Our insane pride tells us it is better to be dead than to admit we can't run our own lives. Many of us continue to prove just that point.

Confusion also results from the amount of value that society in general puts on pride. In reality pride is an inordinate amount of value placed on ones' own importance or dignity. Our distorted thinking in this area is profound. We selectively hear others speak about how important pride is and immediately think that it is something we must have. So we engage in false and misplaced pride to the extent that it makes us miserable at best, and until it kills us at worst.

It's not like the problem with pride is ignored by at least one segment of society. People of deep spiritual convictions often speak about the dangers of pride. After all, it is number one on the list of seven deadly sins. "Pride goes before a fall", as they say. This doesn't mean it leaves, it means it leads the way. Truer words were never spoken when it comes to addiction.

It's not really so surprising that addicts confuse the hell out of recovery. We spend most of our time bullshitting ourselves that using is OK, so when confusion appears in the real world we jump on the bandwagon easily enough.

The plain and simple truth is that our distorted egos won't allow it to be simple. That's why so many of us convince ourselves that pursuing recovery is too hard. Our diseased thinking won't let it come easily. Deep down inside we would still like to have our cake and eat it too. As I said in another chapter, "If I could drink normally, I'd get drunk every night".

CHAPTER 25

Familiar Words, Foreign Concepts

HEARD IN MEETING rooms of recovery: "the good news is that you get your feelings back, the bad news is that you get your feelings back".

As an addict in recovery I now at least have a concept of what remorse, empathy, compassion, and love mean. I associate feelings with them like joy and sadness. I can laugh and truly cry without shame today. Feelings are temporary and come and go without the necessity to act on them or try to obliterate them with drugs. That is progress for me.

The ability to feel negative or positive emotions without having to act on them in a self destructive way is relatively new for me, as it is to most addicts in early recovery. Feelings, especially negative feelings, are a favorite strategy of addicts to have an excuse to use. Positive feelings that are pride based are also an excellent excuse to "celebrate".

The steps and traditions of 12 step recovery permit us to act in a positive manner to help others who reach out for help. Sharing with others about our own ordeals and triumphs passes on to others that they can recover as well. But even more important is the effect it has on our own recovery. "You have to pass it on to keep it", is a well known axiom in working a recovery program. Although any help we try to give others struggling with their disease may or may not be effective, the *effort* to help others helps *us* to stay sober.

Whether helping others acts as a form of atonement for our own past actions, or whether it is a natural progression in pursuing a more spiritual life, it somehow has a positive result for us. More than likely it will also help the fellow addict if they are receptive to accepting help.

Many of the common words and sayings in the rooms of recovery are foreign to addicts even though they sound simple. Most of the meetings I attend start off with a section of the chapter in the Big Book called How it Works. Even though we read that every meeting it is filled with concepts that are hard to practice for addicts. Being honest, thoroughly following someone else's path, being fearless, wanting to be sober, not holding on to old ideas and giving ourselves absolutely to anything are things that we just have not done as practicing addicts. We are pretty much used to doing the opposite of these things.

Given time and with lots of willingness and help from outside ourselves we can begin to understand these concepts. Then we can begin to practice. Any progress in these areas has to be an improvement over the way we have been doing things. Keep in mind we can never be perfect.

CHAPTER 26

Trapped in the Brain of a Bogeyman

OUR ADDICTIVE THINKING leads us to many erroneous conclusions that can lead back to using. For example I can stew in my own juices for a little while and imagine that I am bored. In reality, I have so many options because I am in recovery today that I forget what it was like to have no options. Compared to sitting in a jail cell, the whole world is my playground. I'm not really bored; I just haven't decided which option to take next. If my distorted thinking kicks in and wants to spice things up long enough, I wind up back with no options. That is reality.

Among the options I have are to work in the yard, paddle on the local river, ride my mountain bike, go to the next available recovery meeting, call a troubled fellow addict, clean out the garage, make a piece of hemp jewelry, read, watch a movie, watch TV, walk the dogs, cook, work on a civic project I'm involved with, meditate, listen to music, etc. Because I am an addict and have previously stimulated the pleasure pathway in my brain using chemicals, I can also have the thought that to use again is an option. The reality of where the choice to use leads scares the hell out of me. I am still sick, just not as sick as I used to be because I am aware that my thinking is the bogeyman. The neural connections in my brain which allowed me to use are still in place. They are activated by memories and by feelings. The bridge around them is to not act on the thoughts and surrender to my higher power. Just the knowledge that the imaginary bogeyman is working overtime in my head lets me gladly give up my pride in order to stay sober. I do not have to fight it.

If I were to get pissed off at myself for having the occasional addictive thought it would only generate more negative feelings. I do not have a good track record when confronted with self pity. I've used that excuse as much or more than any other to rationalize that the reward of using was worth the risk. It is much easier to remember the fact that feelings are temporary and that I do not have to react to them.

Continually acknowledging my powerlessness over my thoughts allows me to move on to the business of living. It is the essence of my recovery at this particular point in my journey. If I feel bored it doesn't mean I have to panic today. I may just decide to take a nap and ask my higher power what to do next.

CHAPTER 27

The Present

AT ANY GIVEN moment addicts are in one of three modes: using mode, in recovery, or headed toward a relapse. The difference between the second two is often unclear especially in the mind of the addict. An addict may say they want to stay sober and even think they mean it, but processes in the sub-conscious may be at work to take us back to using behavior. This has happened to me often enough to testify to the truth of it. Further evidence abounds in the rooms of recovery meetings, jails, mental hospitals, and graveyards. These places are filled with people that thought and said they wanted to stay sober and did not. Reality, you can't argue with the truth of it without entering the realm of distorted thinking.

Some people say that the present is a gift, which is why it's called the present. From this moment on our future depends on the decisions we make. This is not a scary proposition if we want to stay sober and have had a psychic change and are removed from the bondage of self. We have all the help we need to make decisions. The hard part is surrendering our pride and seeking help when we need it. For me, as I assume it must be for others in early recovery, I need help often.

The fact that we often make decisions which can begin the process that leads back to using is evidence of the power of the sub-conscious mind. Notice that I said *can* lead back. Clinicians in the field of addiction treatment call these suds (seemingly unimportant decisions). These decisions are usually made based on feelings and what we want. The amount to which these decisions ultimately lead back to using depends on our awareness of when we need help with making decisions. Just like any skill requires practice, we must practice awareness. We must practice until being aware is just part of who we are. Our potential for distorted thinking must be on our mind with any decision we make, no matter how unimportant it may seem. (If you are confused at this point, please go back and read in Chapter 17 about how we have to practice a skill until we do it automatically)

This awareness is the honesty that is mentioned in 12 step recovery programs. The need for this awareness is part of our reality if we want to stay sober. By not being consciously aware at any given moment of our potential for distorted thinking, we return to the bondage of self without realizing it. We are no longer free. We are making decisions based on what our addict brain thinks it wants, and this leads back to using. I simply do not have the power to prevent myself from making poor decisions if I am operating on my own willpower.

If we learn to rely on outside help from our higher power directly and through the suggestions of others in recovery we eventually get to the point where good decisions can be made intuitively. In working the steps of a 12 step recovery program this starts happening around step 9 according to the Big Book of Alcoholics Anonymous. If it does not, then we have missed something in the preceding 8 steps. There is no need to panic about this; we have the rest of our lives to work on it.

Since I have a huge problem with pride, I have not reached this point with just two years of sobriety under my belt. I still sometimes get angry at people and things I cannot control and make decisions based on what I want without considering others or the consequences of my decisions.

At the same time I am grateful that I am aware enough to recognize the emotional pain it causes me when I try to run the show. I may never get to the point where all decisions come intuitively. That would be OK because I am often happy in the present moment by a willingness to reach out for and accept help when I experience emotional pain.

Let me use one example from hundreds I could choose from personally. I left work one day 6 months after drying out in a month long treatment program. I was attending meetings on a regular basis but apparently my sub-conscious mind was not going to the meetings with me. I stopped to get something to eat at a chicken place on the way home. As I parked and got out I decided that I would rather eat at the seafood place almost next to the chicken place. When I say almost, it is because there was a liquor store in between the two. Instead of driving to the seafood place I just walked over. After eating I started back to my car and when I got in front of the liquor store I went in and bought beer on impulse. I didn't even try to think where this decision would lead. It is my belief that I had already relapsed in my sub-conscious mind. The series of seemingly unimportant decisions (suds) which led me to pass in front of the liquor store did not enter my conscious mind as an intentional relapse.

Today, and specifically right at this moment, I know that there are a number of things that can lead me to make poor decisions without consciously acknowledging that I may be doing so. There is a lot of truth to the acronym HALT, (hungry, angry, lonely, tired), playing a part in making poor decisions based on what we feel at the moment. All of these things can make me want to change the way I feel. In my case I have used every feeling a number of times in the past to justify decisions that led

NICHOLAS B.

to that pivotal first drink. Add an S (for sick) to these feelings, give the L double duty (for lust), double duty for T, (thinking I'm tough), and so on. The point is I'm still a sick puppy, no matter what image I think I present to the world.

Through the miracle of my higher power who works through others and who guides me daily I do not want a drink or drug at this moment. Come to think of it, that *is* a gift. I can guarantee you that I did not give this gift to myself.

CHAPTER 28

Beam Me Up Scotty, But Leave Jim Here

ADDICTS OFTEN SUFFER from the problem of perception that just because a treatment method is old and the wording is not modernized that it would not work. Did I mention that this is a perception problem?

The only process for change that works today is the one that has worked throughout history: Not relying on the diseased thinking process. Trying to do this without outside help is impossible. It is a tremendous help to have specific steps to follow that have been time tested by others. As stated previously in the words of Einstein: "The same consciousness that created the problem cannot solve the problem". Yet this reality will continue to trip up addicts unwilling to give up pride and accept outside help either forever or until someone comes up with a cure for the distorted thinking that comes with addiction. (Lobotomies come with too many side effects)

The process of expanding our consciousness to rely on spiritual help is only limited by our pride. With pride in the picture to different degrees in different people, some make the process impossible and some have an easy path. Sometimes there are prejudices that have shaped our beliefs about GOD that have to be overcome. Often our mind will simply not open enough to accept a spiritual attitude toward life. Ironically it is sometimes those with a strict religious background that have more problems than others accepting the diversity of people in the rooms of recovery with all their different beliefs and concepts of a higher power.

The very concept of a spiritual life for me includes not limiting my acceptance of others based on their beliefs. The fact that many diverse concepts provide the help that addicts rely on is proof that a higher power than I can imagine exists. Sometimes I feel that I have been rocketed into the fourth dimension that the Big Book speaks of. I do not feel that way if I set limits on my consciousness.

I mean no offense to anyone named Jim by the title of this chapter, of course. It was just my play on words about Star Trek and the name of bourbon I used to drink by the half gallon. You could say that while I was using, Jim Beam, (or ethyl alcohol in any form), was my higher power. I never have to try and limit the higher power I have today and I don't get the negative consequences from hanging with old Jim.

Diametrically opposed to the way that alcohol obscured my perception, I now derive moments of clarity where reality pours in and makes everything seem brighter than before. With this understanding comes a peace in knowing that everything is happening as it is supposed to without my influence. It was a tough job feeling I had to try to control everything around me. I get to see miracles today instead of being oblivious to them.

CHAPTER 29

The Business of Making Amends

WORKING THE STEPS of a 12 step recovery program includes a process for making amends to those who we harmed with our selfish behavior. Not only is doing this a part of recovery, but there are those who claim that failing to attempt this could cost us our sobriety. I know that it is one of the more difficult parts of recovery for me because of my problem with pride. Humbling myself enough to actually go to a person and lay my part on the line about how I had wronged them is so difficult for me that I cannot do it on my own. I need help with this part of the process from other people as much as my higher power. This means I have to discuss my sins against others and open myself to still more humiliation.

Thank goodness I have help available in the form of other addicts in recovery because it is impossible for me to be accurate in my assessment of actual harm I have caused others. The problem centers on my pride. I can magnify in my mind the harm that I have done as well as minimize my part in causing harm to others. This is because I use distorted thinking both while causing whatever harm there was and also when I think back about the situation.

This part of recovery begins only after we learn to live by not relying on our own thinking to a large degree. We harm ourselves as much as anyone and need to be largely free of the bondage of self before beginning this process. Otherwise we will manage to screw it up because of our inability to look at situations objectively.

To give a brief example from my own life, I got real excited about this making amends business in my first treatment. I couldn't wait to go out and renew old girlfriend acquaintances to make up for the wrongs I had done them. Luckily I brought my plans up in an open meeting. I was properly admonished about how much more harm I could cause by trying to interject myself back into the lives of people who were more than likely just glad to be rid of me and my bullshit. I have since learned that it is less embarrassing to bring such matters up in private with a sponsor or with a counselor.

I also learned in the course of time that the most important amends to make are to those people that I have perhaps harmed the most; family and close friends. These amends can get tricky too. Many of them can best be made by staying sober and honestly trying to live a better life from here on out. While I don't hold with the adage "we only hurt the ones we love", my distorted thinking certainly prevented me from loving anyone unconditionally. My guilt over imagined harm caused me to try and barter material items and "trying to straighten up" for their devotion to me. Many broken promises later, this is finally happening more by default than by me doing anything. GOD is doing for me what I could not do for myself.

Addicts are very adept at manipulating those closest to us. Being engaged in a living amends of practicing unconditional love is hard for most of us but we can do it by living a spiritual life. Real love trumps fear, hate, and all the other negative emotions thrown in together. Not only can I now give it, but I can receive it as well.

CHAPTER 30

The Seeds of the Grapes of Wrath

AN ALTERNATE TITLE to this chapter could be *Misery Loves Company*. Just as there are many good suggestions made in the meeting rooms of recovery, there are many tales of woe that could be filed in our subconscious thinking for our distorted thinking to nurture into rationalizations to use. I have even heard fellow addicts complain that the drinking stories in AA meetings make them thirsty. Obviously they are using that reasoning to justify not going to meetings or actually using. In almost all the meetings I've been to the primary focus has been on following the Steps and the solution instead of dwelling on the problem. If I choose to concentrate on the war stories it is to my own detriment.

The world is full of triggers that distorted thinking can build on. They are present in meetings but mostly in everyday life. If we are unaware of our propensity to rationalize, an afternoon of watching football has us wanting to own a dog named wego that will fetch a beer anytime we yell "here we go". Years ago I just knew the Swedish bikini ski team I saw on beer commercials would rescue me the next time I was drowning in a sea of alcohol. Whenever I entered a bar or social event I told myself I might exit with a member of that team on my arm. I usually ended up drinking myself under the table.

Therefore staying sober is also about how much we are aware that our external environment and the intentions of others can plant seeds for our distorted thinking to nourish. This sounds like repeat information but awareness is so key to sobriety that it cannot be repeated too many times. In this case it is not merely awareness of our own thinking, but also awareness about how outside influences affect us.

When interacting with others, desires and motives are not always communicated or perceived accurately. The meeting rooms are full of people suffering from distorted thinking that finally led them to seek help or as a result of consequences that required them to be at the meeting. Not all people that attend meetings want to stay sober. Some would love to have others join them in their misery. In fact it is not a bit unusual for two people, usually one female and one male, (but not always), to "elope" from recovery into shared misery. Just because we can find someone to validate our bullshit doesn't transform it from bullshit. It just makes it easier to rationalize it. Other addicts are often needy and/or vulnerable and therefore easily taken advantage of. As someone who has enough guilt about the way I used to mislead women as to my intentions, I now use a "look but don't touch" approach. I also have a wife who I love dearly. My wild oat sowing days are over. Undoubtedly age is a factor as well, but mostly it is the fact that I don't want to cause harm to others today with selfish motives. My lust was a product of off-the-chain pride.

There can also be an element of danger in the way we attempt to help others. It is OK to reach out a helping hand to those still suffering, but it is harmful to us if we bolster our pride with it. It is also easy to feel we are inadequate if the person we are attempting to help does not accept it. This may happen repeatedly with several different people not accepting offered help. The catchy slogan in AA is "you can carry the message, but you can't carry the drunk". It is possible to become so enmeshed in another addict's problems that we shift the focus off of our own recovery and return to distorted thinking.

CHAPTER 31

No Need to Fear

THE ONLY LEGITIMATE fear is the fear that we are born with. At first, because we don't have awareness of what things will do to us we fear things that cause physical pain. As we experience life we learn what things hurt us, emotionally and physically. At some point in time, children realize that life will come to an end for them by observing it happen to others. Fear of dying and physical pain are based on reality. Only by developing a sense of self do we begin adding emotional fears associated with not getting what we want.

Masking fear is, in my opinion, one reason addicts begin using and continue to use. Selfish fears of not getting what we want or losing something we think we have are very real to us. By reacting to these selfish fears in self destructive ways we usually do lose things and end up not getting what we want in the process. The fact that we use to the point of killing ourselves or putting ourselves through severe emotional pain shows just how sick we really are. Addicts commit suicide by using if it is not stopped by recovery or incarceration. Jails and mental hospitals often become our home away from home.

Since certain eventual death is the thing we can least control, it is ironic although not surprising that we self centered addicts need help outside of ourselves to live in the real world. Our concept of the world has been limited to the perception that it is up to us to control rather than accept reality. Our thinking is so distorted that we actually head toward the thing that we should legitimately fear most.

Self proclaimed daredevil and adrenaline junkie notwithstanding, I have less fear of death today because I am in recovery. This is partly because I am putting myself in less danger of dying sooner rather than later. It is also because I can accept my own death as part of my spiritual journey. The power that created me made death a part of my existence. Any fear associated with dying is natural and only the undertaking of a spiritual journey will help me to understand and accept it. Artificially numbing my brain to become oblivious to it only makes it more nightmarish in between blackouts or passing outs. Using immediately cuts off all hope of a conscious contact with my higher power which is the source of help I need to cope with fear. Trying to deny legitimate fear is a futile exercise which only leads to using to help forget about it.

In the real world, (not the world of my distorted thinking), things happen as they are supposed to when they are supposed to. I cannot change them and worrying about them makes living in the present less enjoyable.

The mystery of why we were created will remain a mystery. The living is in being grateful for the fact that we *were* created in the first place and to experience what life has to offer without harming ourselves and others. It certainly isn't in doing something to end our existence or make ourselves miserable because of our own selfish pride. As the old saying goes: GOD didn't make junk.

THE LAST CHAPTER

MY JOURNEY THUS far has taken 60 years plus. I feel I have struck the tip of an iceberg of knowledge that I will continue to explore as I continue my journey. The amount that I don't know about living a spiritual life keeps growing which I hope means that I will remain teachable.

Whether I stay sober or not is immaterial for anybody else's journey. This is being written during a period of my journey in which I am experiencing sobriety and the resulting benefits. I have empathy for all addicts I come in contact with. I can also show love in a committed relationship with my partner who is my role model of faith and devotion. Because of her unshakable faith in *her* higher power, I bear witness each day to the power of faith. And that is something worth living for.

In the introduction of this book I mentioned that my opinions are my own, but our powerlessness is as real as gravity. I can choose to accept it or reject it. For most of my life I rejected it. This resulted in many self made problems. The same power that created me and allowed me to use my self will almost to the point of self destruction also allows me to stay in recovery and gives me freedom from the bondage of self. Today I hold no resentments toward that power. Today using that power is a matter of life and death as it always was. It is just that I am aware of it today and don't reject it. Just for today and just for the moment I allow myself to reach out for and accept help. Today I can plug into it.

My significant Other just reminded me that I have responsibilities besides sitting on my butt in front of a computer. A final acronym to help remember the qualities we need for recovery. HOW: Honesty, Open-mindedness, and Willingness.